Money Is an Art

100 Quotes for Designing Your Financial Landscape

J.B. Waters

"Our financial landscape is a blank canvas; each choice is a brushstroke that can create a masterpiece or result in a failed work. These 100 quotes will help you design a financial future that reflects your true desires. Let's create the masterpiece you deserve."
- J.B. Waters

Money Is an Art

100 Quotes for Designing Your Financial Landscape

Copyright © 2024 by J.B. Waters
www.jbwaters.com

All rights reserved.
No portion of this book may be reproduced in any form
without written permission from the publisher or author,
except for the use of brief quotations in a book review.

The information in this book is not financial advice, and
you should not consider it to be financial advice.

Printed in the United States of America
Cover Design: J.B. Waters
Illustrations: J.B, Waters

First Printing, 2024
Published by 1888 House LLC

ISBN 978-1-7373645-4-2

Money Is an Art

100 Quotes for Designing Your Financial Landscape

J.B. Waters

Wealth starts in the mind

Know the numbers

Being broke is selfish

Time isn't money

Money is energy

Money cares for those who care for it

Money is a magnifying glass

It takes emotion to make money and logic to keep it

The cost of spending money is freedom

Your money goes in the same direction as you

This book features 100 quotes, including 10 Core quotes, each with a related subcore quote.

I hope these 10 pictures inspire you to come up with ten thousand ways to make money—just one great idea is all you need.

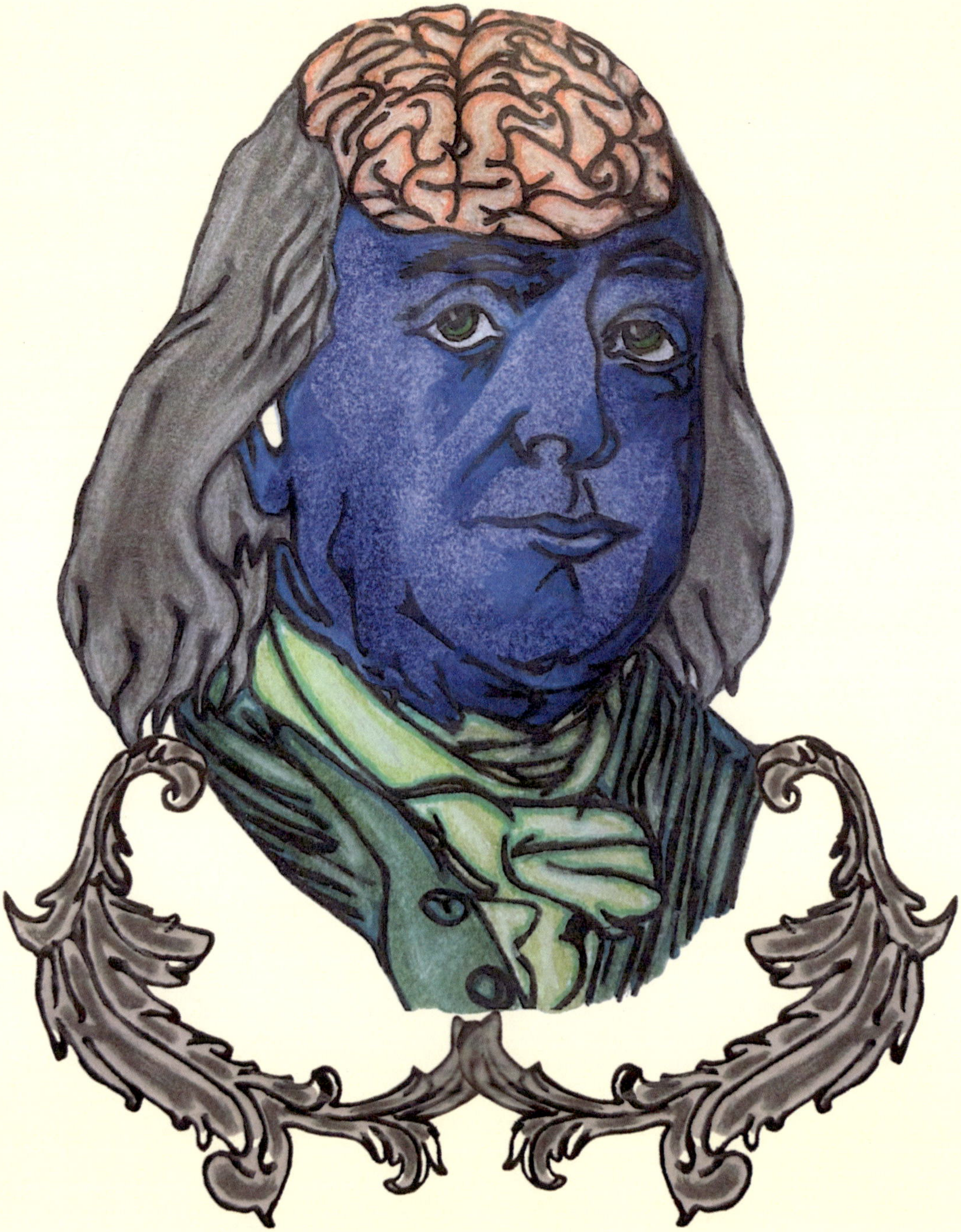

Wealth starts in the mind.

Money doesn't exist without an idea to spend it on.

Cash was created to create with.

Your thoughts can be expensive or profitable.

Every thought has a price tag.

Your mind is the safest place to store your money.

The more you use your thoughts to make money,
the less you think about making money.

The tangible is a child of the invisible.

Worry about losing your mind, not your money.

Your mind isn't the best place for your ideas.

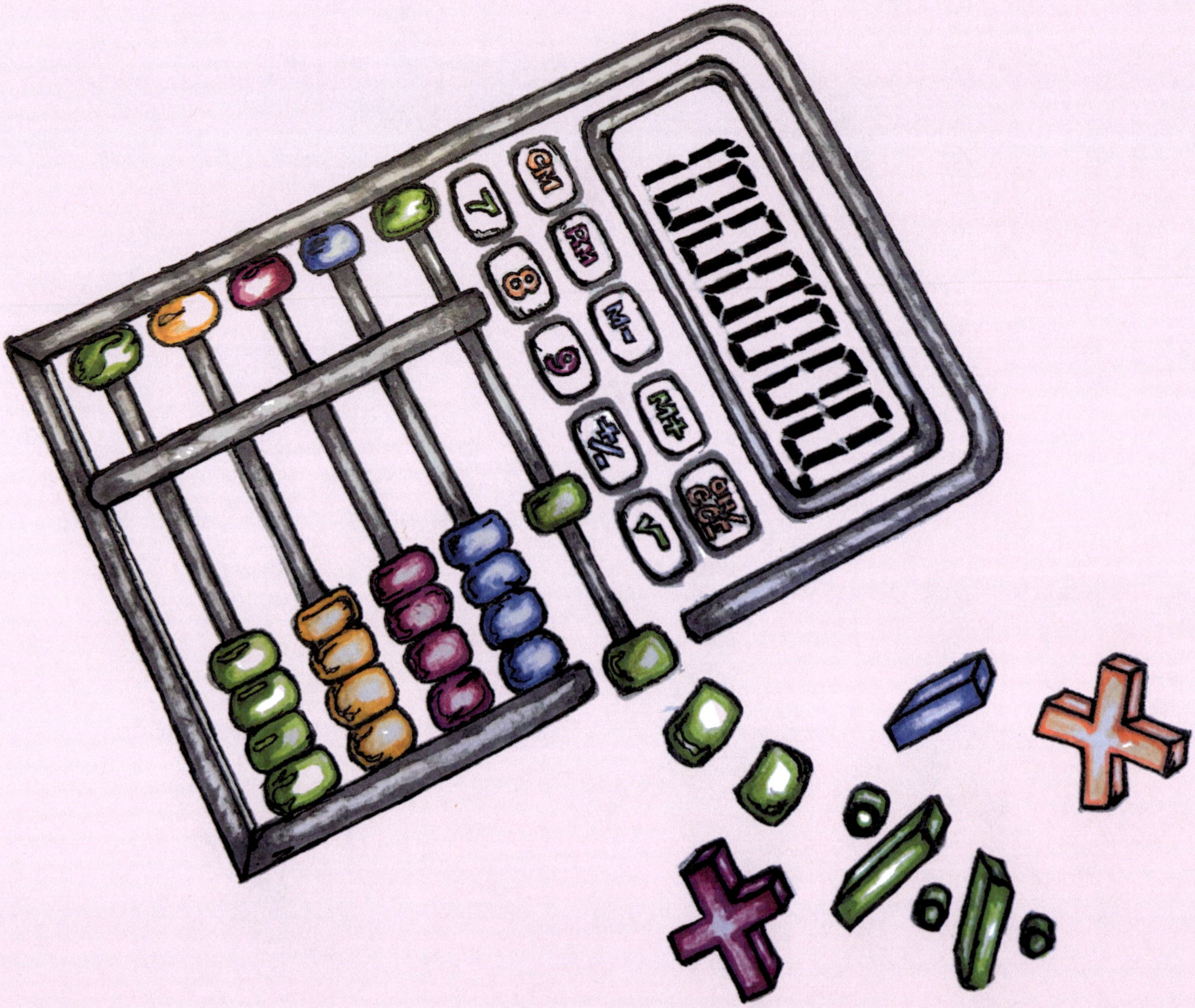

KNOW THE NUMBERS.

Do the math on all areas that involve financial transactions.

Know the pennies, so it's easier to know the dollars.

Forgetting to count the number is worse than not having the number.

The numbers are a reminder.

10% percent of something is better than 100% of nothing.

Know personal expenses so you eventually only care about your business expenses.

If numbers don't lie, then make sure you know the truth about yours.

The right usage of paper and ink creates more paper and ink.

Make sure every dollar has a job.

Place yourself in a position financially to help others.

You can help more people with money than without it.

Write down a list of people you think money can help and serve.

You can't give what you don't have.

Having just enough only helps you.

There's a reason why you're not alone on earth,
and that reason is to serve.

We are the result of everyone who contributed before us.

Is the life you have worth offering to someone else?

Your lack affects those around you as much as it does you.

Time Isn't Money.

You can get money back, but you can't get time back.

Being intentional with your time allows you not to regret your choices.

Time is a rarer resource than money.

Yesterday is one of many, but tomorrow is one of none.

The past is gone, and tomorrow is uncertain—so prepare for the unknown.

What's worse, wasted time or wasted money?

Time is the real value of money.

When you start matters.

The only way to get more time is to get more money.

Concentration requires energy, and money follows attention and focus.

Your energy is focused on making money when your body is present to earn it.

Currency grows when it moves and flows like a current.

Money follows feelings.

Consider how much energy was put into
your money when it goes out.

How tired you are after you make money
is a good sign of your financial state.

Giving and receiving should equally feel good.

Having money takes and gives, but not having money only takes.

Money is the transferring of energy disguised.

MONEY CARES FOR THOSE WHO CARE FOR IT.

Don't be the reason you and money have a toxic relationship.

The moment you forget about money, money forgets about you.

Reliable, realistic, resourceful, and rich all begin with the letter R.

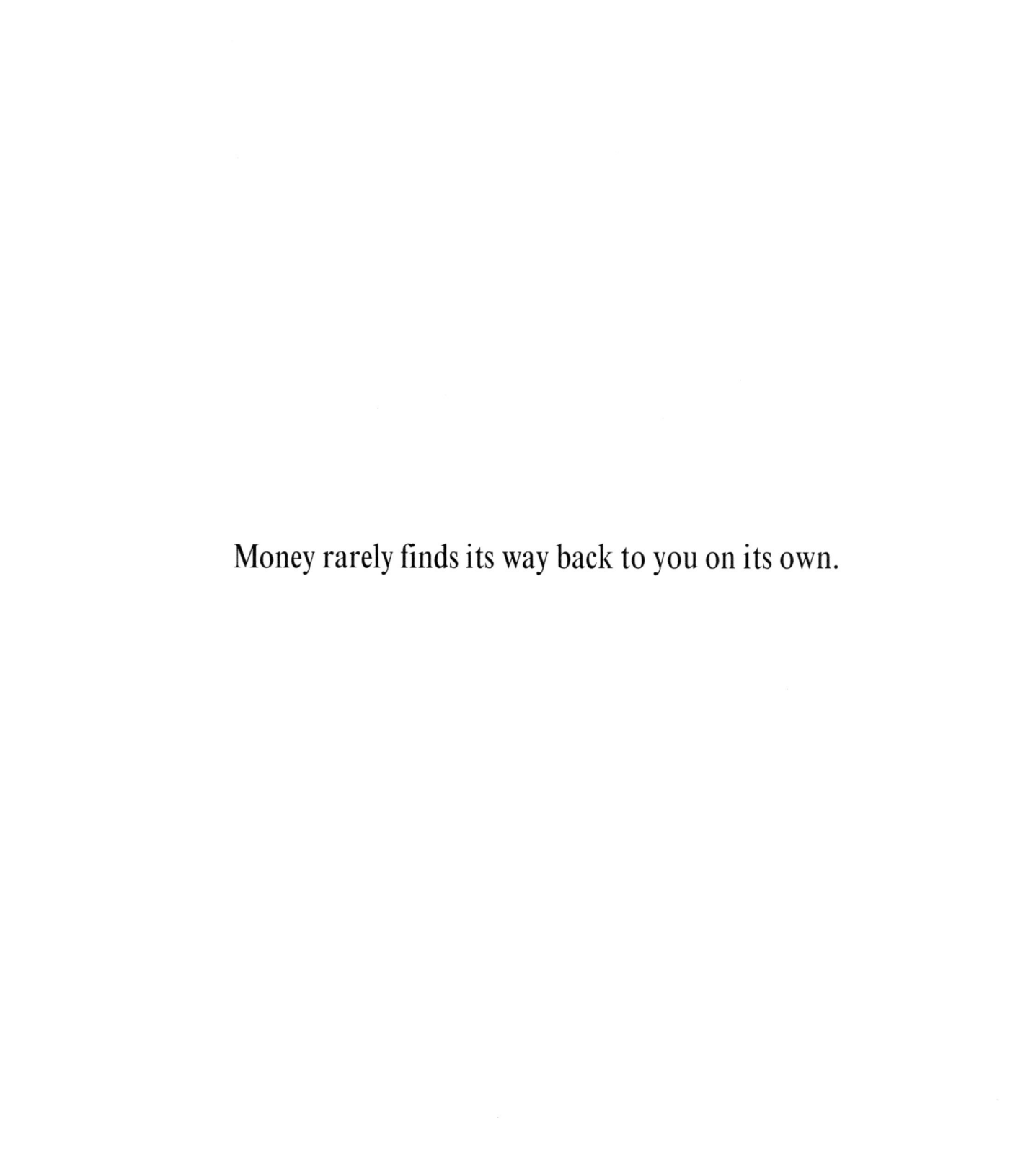

Money rarely finds its way back to you on its own.

Pay bills with a smile because services are rendered with a smile.

When you save money, money saves you.

Most people's money is better off in someone else's hands.

As a parent, how often did you not know where your child was?

How much money you have directly reflects how much you care about it.

Whatever you are without money, you will be even more with it.

Money doesn't build discipline; it reveals discipline.

Learn to say no to yourself without money because you hear it less when you have money.

The things you have today are the result of the person you were yesterday.

To see someone's true colors, observe what they spend money on.

Money can hide what people see but not what people feel.

If you pay attention, you'll notice that every dollar has a story.

Ask for something without money, and you'll reveal what you truly seek with it.

Your possessions reveal your inner self.

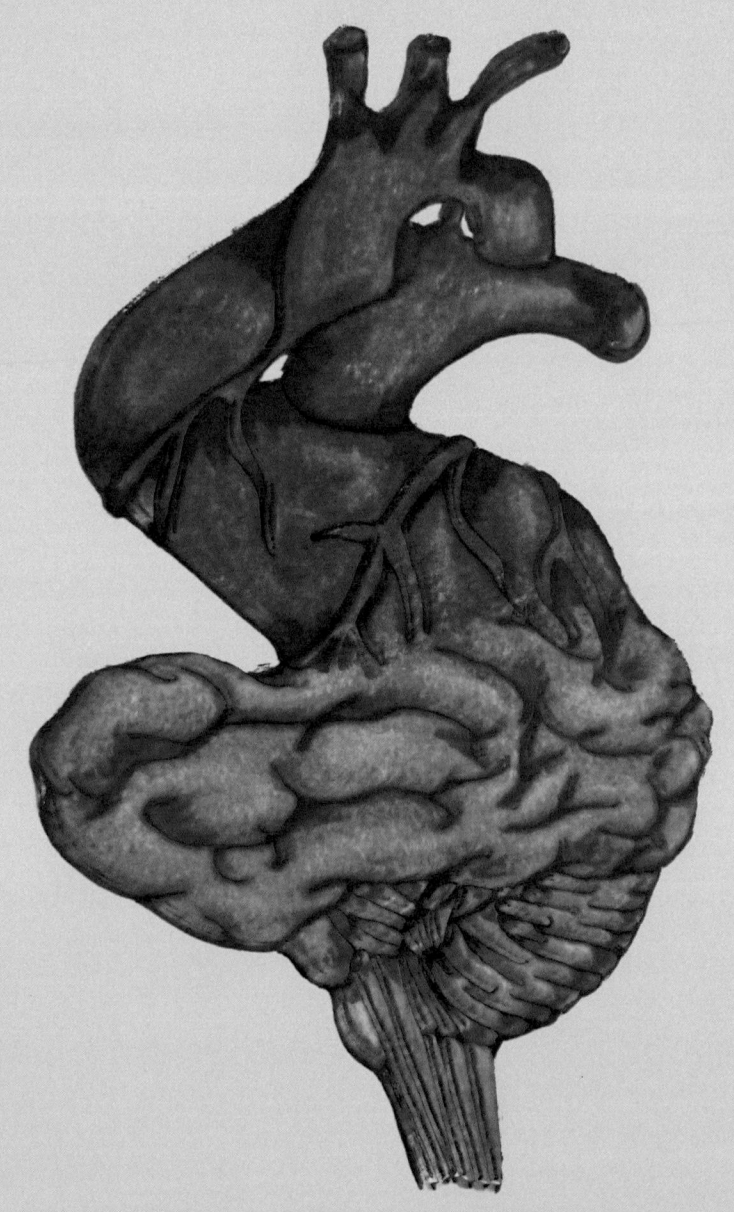

IT TAKES EMOTION TO MAKE MONEY AND LOGIC TO KEEP IT.

Use your passion to fuel your ideas.

Desire is the fire that lights the way to income.

Separately, the heart and hand can always hurt money,
but together, they can always help money.

Consumption and production can be logical
or emotional, depending on the person.

Receive income, count to 60, then decide whether to spend it.

Boring income can lead to exciting expenses.

Patience paired with persistence yields the greatest return.

You won't see the passion in your plan initially.

Financial investments are logical, but companies thrive on emotions.

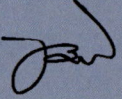

The cost of spending money is freedom.

The money you spend today will either free or enslave you tomorrow.

Until your future expenses are covered by your current income, you'll always be spending tomorrow's money.

Your money shouldn't require your presence.

Less money leaves you with the leftovers.

Options are a by-product of money.

Being negligent with money is being indifferent to your freedom.

Spending money is either the key to your freedom or the lock on your chain.

You're paying for freedom by buying back your time.

View every dollar as an amount of freedom you can access.

Your money goes in the same direction as you.

The seeds of your money tree grow with knowledge and consistent execution.

Bad fruit comes from bad roots.

Your finances are a direct reflection of your philosophy.

You don't have money problems; you have character problems.

The direction of your financial compass will determine your destination.

Compounded good choices are better than compound interest.

Appreciation appreciates.

Each dollar you spend lays a brick on the path to growth or regression.

Make sure your money arrives at the destination before you do.

I hope the quotes and principles in this book help you create a financial masterpiece you're proud to share. Remember, each choice is a brushstroke on your financial canvas, and only you can shape the outcome. With love and faith, stay well and mindful.
Your ally and friend,
Julian.

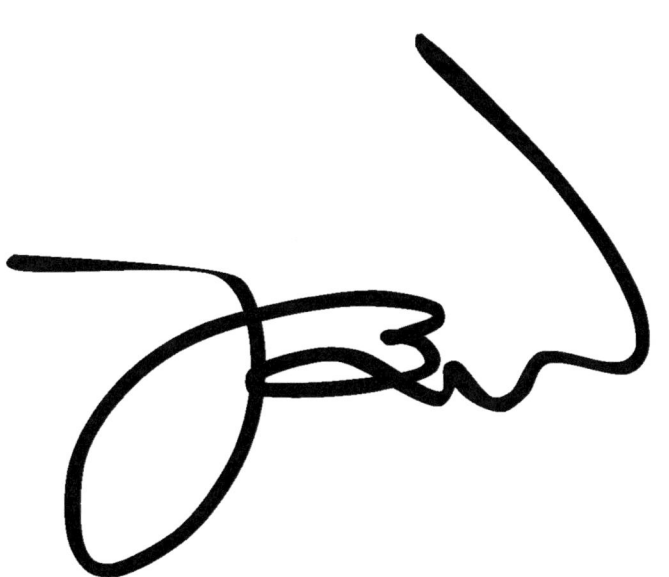

www.ingramcontent.com/pod-product-compliance
Lightning Source LLC
Chambersburg PA
CBRC091454160426
43209CB00024B/1890